The Waco Siege: The History of the Federal Government's Standoff with David Koresh and the Branch Davidians

By Charles River Editors

A picture of the Mount Carmel Center on fire during the siege

About Charles River Editors

Charles River Editors provides superior editing and original writing services across the digital publishing industry, with the expertise to create digital content for publishers across a vast range of subject matter. In addition to providing original digital content for third party publishers, we also republish civilization's greatest literary works, bringing them to new generations of readers via ebooks.

Sign up here to receive updates about free books as we publish them, and visit Our Kindle Author Page to browse today's free promotions and our most recently published Kindle titles.

Introduction

Picture of a tank breaking down one of the compound's walls

The Siege of Waco (1993)

*Includes pictures

*Includes accounts of the standoff by federal agents and members of the Branch Davidians

*Includes online resources and a bibliography for further reading

*Includes a table of contents

"If you are a Branch Davidian, Christ lives on a threadbare piece of land 10 miles east of here called Mount Carmel. He has dimples, claims a ninth-grade education, married his legal wife when she was 14, enjoys a beer now and then, plays a mean guitar, reportedly packs a 9mm Glock and keeps an arsenal of military assault rifles, and willingly admits that he is a sinner without equal." – The opening passage of "The Sinful Messiah", published in the *Waco Tribune-Herald* on February 27, 1993

"I am more willing to come out when I get my message from my commander." – David Koresh

In February 1993, President Bill Clinton had only been in office for a few weeks when one of the most important events of his presidency began to take shape. Ironically, it would involve a group that the vast majority of Americans had never heard of and knew absolutely nothing about.

The Branch Davidians were an obscure religious sect located in Texas, but members of the group led by David Koresh in Waco, Texas stockpiled enough weaponry to catch the attention of the federal government. The U.S. Bureau of Alcohol, Tobacco, Firearms and Explosives (ATF) ultimately decided to serve arrest and search warrants at the compound for the possession of illegal weapons, even though they fully expected it would require a raid that could potentially turn fatal.

The ATF hoped to use the element of surprise when it commenced the raid on February 28, but the Branch Davidians were ready for them, which led to an intense firefight between the two sides that resulted in the deaths of 4 ATF agents and a number of Branch Davidians. With that, the FBI got involved, and federal agents settled in for a standoff that would last about 50 days, trying everything from negotiating to using sleep deprivation tactics to coerce the Branch Davidians into ending the confrontation. Finally, on April 19, government agents breached the compound's walls and tried to use gas to flush the Branch Davidians out peacefully, but a series of fires broke out and quickly spread, killing the vast majority of the occupants inside, including many young children.

Naturally, controversy spread over how the siege ended; for example, while most believe the Branch Davidians intentionally started the fires as part of a mass suicide, others insist it was the fault of the ATF. Debate also raged over whether the government could have and should have made different decisions to defuse the situation. As Alan Stone put it in a study of the siege, "The tactical arm of federal law enforcement may conventionally think of the other side as a band of criminals or as a military force or, generically, as the aggressor. But the Branch Davidians were an unconventional group in an exalted, disturbed, and desperate state of mind. They were devoted to David Koresh as the Lamb of God. They were willing to die defending themselves in an apocalyptic ending and, in the alternative, to kill themselves and their children. However, these were neither psychiatrically depressed, suicidal people nor cold-blooded killers. They were ready to risk death as a test of their faith. The psychology of such behavior—together with its religious significance for the Branch Davidians—was mistakenly evaluated, if not simply ignored, by those responsible for the FBI strategy of 'tightening the noose'. The overwhelming show of force was not working in the way the tacticians supposed. It did not provoke the Branch Davidians to surrender, but it may have provoked David Koresh to order the mass-suicide." In 1999, a report prepared by the federal government itself concluded, "The violent tendencies of dangerous cults can be classified into two general categories—defensive violence and offensive violence. Defensive violence is utilized by cults to defend a compound or enclave that was created specifically to eliminate most contact with the dominant culture. The 1993 clash in Waco, Texas at the Branch Davidian complex is an illustration of such defensive violence. History has shown that groups that seek to withdraw from the dominant culture seldom act on their beliefs that the endtime has come unless provoked."

No matter which side people came down on, the violent confrontation embarrassed government officials, and Dick Morris, an advisor of Clinton's, even claimed that Attorney General Janet Reno only kept her job after Waco by threatening to pin the blame on the president: "[H]e went into a meeting with her, and he told me that she begged and pleaded, saying that . . . she didn't want to be fired because if she were fired it would look like he was firing her over Waco. And I knew that what that meant was that she would tell the truth about what happened in Waco. Now, to be fair, that's my supposition. I don't know what went on in Waco, but that was the cause. But I do know that she told him that if you fire me, I'm going to talk about Waco."

In addition to influencing how the government approached potential future conflicts with other groups, Waco's most important legacy was that it enraged people who already had an anti-government bent. The most notable, of course, was Timothy McVeigh, who conducted what was at the time the deadliest terrorist attack in American history in Oklahoma City on the second anniversary of the final confrontation at Waco.

The Waco Siege: The History of the Federal Government's Standoff with David Koresh and the Branch Davidians chronicles the controversial event and the influence it had. Along with pictures of important people, places, and events, you will learn about Waco like never before, in no time at all.

The Waco Siege: The History of the Federal Government's Standoff with David Koresh and the Branch Davidians

About Charles River Editors

Introduction

    Chapter 1: I Got to Know David

    Chapter 2: Just Bible Students

    Chapter 3: Guns Blazing

    Chapter 4: Under Siege for 51 Days

    Chapter 5: The Tanks Rolled In

    Chapter 6: Questions

    Online Resources

    Bibliography

Chapter 1: I Got to Know David

"Back in 1990 I had been drumming in a local rock band. I needed some new sticks, and on the way to a gig stopped in at the music store. Seeing the sticks in my hand, two strangers introduced themselves and asked if I was in a band. The two were Koresh and Steve Schneider. Schneider gave me his card and I handed it back. The backside was full of Bible verses. 'You guys are a Christian band,' I said, uninterested. But after some small talk, I took the card back, and a few days later gave him a call. Over the next few weeks I hung out with Koresh and some other musicians in his band. I got to know David and was somewhat impressed. Having never paid much attention to the Bible, I was astonished to find that it actually did have some relevance to my life." - David Thibodeaux, one of the survivors

Prior to 1993, few people outside of Waco, Texas had heard of the Branch Davidians, and most of those who had wrote them off as just another strange religious cult. In fact, the group initially formed during the Great Depression as Shepherd's Rod after breaking off from the Seventh-Day Adventist Church. When the cult's founder, Victor Houteff, died in 1955, the group expanded, moving to the Waco, Texas area. Benjamin Roden took over leadership of the group in 1959, and he remained in charge until he died, at which point his wife Lois took control. She groomed a young man named Vernon Howell to take her place. In 1984, the group split again and Howell moved with his people to Palestine, Texas, while the rest stayed in Waco with George Roden, Benjamin and Lois' son.

Houteff

Benjamin Roden

Lois Roden

George Roden

Following Lois' death in January 1987, George Roden and Howell sparred over who should get possession of the Mount Carmel Center. According to a story published a few years later, "Roden dug up the body of Anna Hughes from the cemetery at Mount Carmel, storing the casket inside a shed. Roden then issued a challenge to Howell: the man who raised Hughes from the dead would be the Branch Davidians' true prophet. Howell and his followers asked the McLennan County Sheriff's Department to arrest Roden for corpse abuse. Officials demanded proof, such as a photograph of Hughes' body. Howell and seven men, all dressed in camouflage fatigues, sneaked into Mount Carmel on Nov. 3, 1987, supposedly to take such a photograph. They carried assault rifles. When daylight came, a shootout ensued. Deputies, notified by neighbors, broke up the skirmish. They filed charges of attempted murder against Howell and his followers. Although the Branch Davidians claimed to be carrying weapons for protection, they had put 18 bullet holes into the small tree Roden hid behind."

The trial was notorious and brought the Branch Davidians unwanted publicity that no doubt contributed to their downfall just a few years later. The story continued, "Howell's followers clogged the third floor of the McLennan County Courthouse for the trial. Most of the women wore dresses to their ankles and blouses buttoned up to their necks. They clamored around their men during breaks. Children clung tightly to their mothers. Roden, the prosecution's chief witness, came to the courtroom straight from the county jail, where he was serving a six-month sentence for filing legal motions asking God to inflict AIDS and herpes on Texas Supreme Court judges. Before the trial started, visiting Judge Herman Fitts asked if there were any witnesses in the courtroom who needed to be sworn in. No one arose. Howell's attorney Gary Coker intervened. He turned to Branch Davidians in the gallery, urging potential witnesses to stand. Again no one got up. Howell, smiling slightly, then stood. 'It's all right,' he said, raising a hand. 'You've done nothing wrong. Stand.' The doubt parted and the witnesses stood. In his testimony, Roden told of trying to raise Hughes from the dead and with not a hint of chagrin, admitted ending a prayer, 'In the name of George B. Roden, amen.' The jury acquitted Howell's followers. It could not reach a verdict on Howell. Charges against him were later dropped. With Roden in jail, the Branch Davidians settled back into Mount Carmel."

Once back in Waco, Howell acted quickly to solidify authority over his followers by striking at the very heart of their personal lives with his "New Light" tapes, released on August 9, 1989. In them, he claimed that God had told him to take the women, even the married ones, of the group and have children with them. Meanwhile, their husbands would remain celibate.

Needless to say, this had the effect of separating the true believers from the rest. Howell went on to tell them, "Only the Lamb is to be given the job to raise up the seed of the House of David, isn't he? ... You [women] have only one seen that can deliver you from death...There's only one hard-on in this whole universe that really loves you and wants to say good things about you. Remember Mary and God? Yeah? God couldn't make any advances because the world would misjudge. ... If the Bible is true, then I'm Christ. But so what? Look at 2,000 years ago. What's so great about being Christ? A man nailed to the cross. A man of sorrow acquainted with grief. You know, being Christ ain't nothing. Know what I mean?...If the Bible is true, I'm Christ. If the Bible is true. But all I want out of this is for people to be honest this time. ... God allows men to be born into sin. It is natural for man to sin. If you're going to be fair, you've got to give man a way out."

In the summer of 1990, Howell legally changed his name to David Koresh, a change that was supposed to symbolize to his followers a connection to two Old Testament figures. David symbolized a lineage to King David, from whom the Messiah would come, while Koresh is the Persian name of Cyrus the Great, the Persian king seen as a messiah figure because he allowed the Jews to return to the land of Israel after the Babylonian captivity. By changing his name to David Koresh, he was professing to his followers that he was the spiritual descendant of the biblical David and, therefore, the Messiah.

Koresh

Such was his control over his followers that they accepted Koresh's claim. Livingstone Fagan was one of the believers who survived, and he remained faithful to Koresh's teachings long after the siege was over and the smoke had cleared. He later wrote, "David Koresh is Messiah, being first amongst men to be born into God Consciousness. Having been born under the first creation into this consciousness, he was established as a sign post (sic) before this creation, to show Adam's race a way out should they fall short of the standard set at the beginning. Hence the phrase "the Lamb slain from the foundation of the earth." As a matter of fact, Adam was created like unto God the Son at the conclusion of the first creation, which is the material image of God. God the Son, of the first creation, has been raised up from death for the salvation of man. This time however he is to be made Messiah over the coming kingdom of God on earth. The Spirit of God is to dwell in all its citizens."

Chapter 2: Just Bible Students

"That fall I went to Waco to play music and meet the larger community. The people at Mount Carmel were extremely involved in knowing and learning the Bible. People have made it seem as if Mount Carmel came out of nowhere. In fact, Koresh was the third leader of a community that spun off from the Seventh Day Adventists in the 1930s. They had been living outside of Waco since 1933. The people around Koresh came from many backgrounds. One irony of Waco is that right-wing extremists and racists look to Mount Carmel as a beacon. If they realized that so many of us were black, Asian and Latino, and that we despised their hateful politics and anger, they would probably feel betrayed. We weren't political at all – just Bible students. We had a 'live and let live' attitude that had allowed us to get along well with our neighbors for over 60 years. We certainly weren't as isolated as people seem to think. We shopped in town, worked in the community, and our band played weekend gigs in Waco nightclubs. I worked as a bartender in Waco and I doubt a single customer would tell you that I stood out in any way."

In 1992, Koresh sold most of the group's land around Waco and kept only 77 acres, which he fortified with increased security measures. By this time, there were multiple generations living on the compound, including young adults who knew of no other life. Nonetheless, those living in and around the compound slowly became aware that there was something strange going on at "Mount Carmel," which had been named after a mountain in Israel considered sacred in the Old Testament. Bob Lott, the City Editor for the *Waco Tribune Herald*, later observed, "[His followers] truly believe that he was the messiah. ... And his role was to open the seven seals that are mentioned in the Book of Revelation. He had what was called his new light revelation and that was that as the messiah, he should generate a new population of people to inherent the kingdom of God and to do that all of the women in the group belonged to him." One survivor, Clive Doyle, agreed, saying, "He began to present the ideas that he had and I'd say 99 percent of the leadership of the church that were living at Mount Carmel accepted him as having a message from God. ... David was constantly talking to God. God told me to do this. God told me to do that. And we accepted that. ... The men in the group would choose to become celibate. And if they were married, they would, you know, not have any more relations with their wives. ... When David first started teaching, he began to show that God asked prophets to do what we might consider strange things a lot of times."

Not surprisingly, Koresh told a different but equally disturbing version of the story: "God speaks to me. I have a message to present. ... I mean, there are some things that God has concealed in his written word that are to be brought to do right before the end of time. ... It's true. I do have a lot of children. And it's true I do have a lot of wives. I mean, I just -- it is my great, wonderful looks, something that women can't resist."

However, it wasn't just the number of wives he had; it was the age they were when he "married" them. Lott explained, "We had evidence that he had sexually abused girls as young as 12. We also discovered that that had been going on for a couple of years and law enforcement had not done anything really to prevent it or stop it."

Concerned, Lott assigned two reporters, Mark England and Darlene McCormick, to investigate the accusations. After eight months following the story, the two reported their findings in a series of seven articles published in the *Tribune-Herald* in February 1993. In the paper, the two turned a harsh spotlight on group: "If you are a Branch Davidian, Christ lives on a threadbare piece of land 10 miles east of here called Mount Carmel. He has dimples, claims a ninth-grade education, married his legal wife when she was 14, enjoys a beer now and then, plays a mean guitar, reportedly packs a 9mm Glock and keeps an arsenal of military assault rifles, and willingly admits that he is a sinner without equal. David Koresh is now his legal name. He changed it two years ago in California, supposed to enhance his career as a musician. To former cult members and law enforcement authorities, though, he is still Vernon Howell. Many of Howell's followers are former Seventh-day Adventists. The Seventh-day Adventist Church strongly denies any connection with Howell's group. Howell's followers have come to 77 acres near the Elk community from Australia, New Zealand, Canada, England, Hawaii and throughout the continental United States. The end of the world is near, they believe. Howell, 33, is their salvation. … Although many followers have fled, Howell remains with about 75 faithful in a compound they built to await the end of the world. Former cult members and authorities say it is heavily armed. Guards reportedly walked the grounds at night. Perched above the compound is a tower with lookout windows facing all directions."

The articles went on to accuse Koresh and other leaders of the cult of gross and violent abuse against children. According to the reporters, Koresh was a polygamist who regularly "married" underage girls and claimed to be entitled to sexual favors from any female living in the compound. These accusations were backed up by an anonymous woman who said,"[Koresh] was supposed to be the son of God. He said God was really lonesome, and he wanted grandchildren. It was like the Scriptures kind of said it, but they didn't really. It was like he was giving God grandchildren."

While the allegations made in the articles were horrific, they had been made against numerous cult leaders in the past. Instead, what set Koresh apart was the fact that the paper reported the Branch Davidians also had stockpiles of weapons. These rumors came courtesy of a UPS driver who was delivering a package that broke open and contained a number of weapons, including unarmed grenades and black powder. On July 9, 1992, the ATF opened an investigation into these claims and to others made by people who claimed they had heard what sounded like automatic gunfire coming from the compound. A member of the Branch Davidians, Marc Breault, later admitted that Koresh indeed had the parts necessary to convert regular guns into automatic weapons, which was in clear violation of the Hughes Amendment of the Firearm Owners Protection Act of 1986.

In the course of the investigation, FBI Agent Randy Parsons summarized what the government discovered: "They had acquired…weapons, rifles, pistols, shotguns, grenades, grenade launchers. Almost two million rounds of ammunition. A fully automatic rifle is, of course, illegal to possess." David Aguilera, an agent with the ATF, was assigned to investigate and later recalled, "I was discovering a lot of AR-15s. They were converting these weapons from semiautomatic to automatic weapons. I was outraged and I was able to go out and get enough probable cause to make sure that, you know, I'm going to get my warrant for this guy."

The ATF sent a surveillance team to rent a house across the road from the compound in January 1993. The agents posed as college students and sent one man to "meet the neighbors." Aguilera explained, "We had an undercover agent, Special Agent Robert Rodriguez, who actually had interaction and met with David Koresh. He says, you know, I don't care what the ATF says or does. It's my right to -- you know, to bear weapons, and nobody is ever going to take me down. That's a red flag."

A bunch of 30-something guys sharing a house and claiming to be college students struck Koresh as suspicious, and he stopped leaving the compound as he had regularly used to do. By then, however, the agents had enough information to obtain search warrants for the compound and an arrest warrant for the cult leader himself. On February 25, 1993, Aguilera presented U.S. Magistrate Dennis Green with an affidavit stating that the Branch Davidians had purchased a large number of legal gun parts that he felt could be used to create illegal weapons. "As a result of my training and experience as a Special Agent for the Bureau of Alcohol, Tobacco and Firearms, I am familiar with the Federal firearm and explosive laws and know that it is unlawful for a person to manufacture, possess, transfer, or to transport or ship in interstate commerce machine guns, machine gun conversion parts, or explosives which are classified, by Federal law, as machine guns, and/or destructive devices, including any combination of parts either designed or intended for use in converting any firearm into a machine gun, or into a destructive device as defined by Federal law, and from which a destructive device may be readily assembled, without them being lawfully registered in the National Firearms Registration and Transfer Record, U.S. Treasury Department, Washington, D.C. During my 5 years' experience with the Bureau of Alcohol, Tobacco and Firearms, I have investigated persons who have unlawfully possessed, transferred or shipped in interstate or foreign commerce firearms and/or explosive devices which were not registered to them with the National Firearms Registration and Transfer Record, and have successfully participated in the prosecution of several of these individuals."

In addition to telling the court about all the investigations and interviews he had performed himself, Aguilera related a very disturbing tale told to investigators by a social worker with the Texas Department of Human Services, Joyce Sparks. "Ms. Sparks said that she noticed a trap door in the floor at one end of the building. When she inquired about it, Koresh allowed her to look into the trap door. She could see a ladder leading down into a buried school bus from which all the seats had been removed. At one end of the bus she could see a very large refrigerator with numerous bullet holes. She also saw three long guns lying on the floor of the bus, however, she did not know the make or caliber of them. She stated that there was no electricity in the bus. Everything she saw was with the aid of a pen light. When questioned by Ms. Sparks, Koresh said that the bus was where he practiced his target shooting in order not to disturb his neighbors. ... When she asked to speak with some of the children and other residents, Koresh refused, stating they were not available. She said that during her conversation with Koresh, he told her that he was the 'Messenger' from God, that the world was coming to an end, and that when he 'reveals' himself the riots in Los Angeles would pale in comparison to what was going to happen in Waco,

Texas. Koresh stated that it would be a 'military type operation' and that all the 'non-believers' would have to suffer."

Chapter 3: Guns Blazing

"Many have suggested that Koresh was a Jim Jones-like madman. He wasn't. He had no plans for mass suicide. In contrast to Jones, Koresh allowed members to leave at any time, and many of them did, even during the siege. But many stayed, too, not because we had to, but because we wanted to. We felt the FBI and ATF had been dishonest from the start. Few Americans realize that on February 28, 1993 when ATF agents in National Guard helicopters zoomed in on Mount Carmel Center, they did so with guns blazing. The initial raid, in which four ATF agents and six Davidians were killed, was a publicity stunt for the 20/20 television show, who were there to document it. ATF employees would later admit the underlying charges were 'a complete fabrication.' Everyone knew David Koresh hated drugs. Charges that we were assembling an arsenal of weapons to be used against the government were equally off-base. We had nothing to hide. In fact, weeks before the raid, Koresh offered the ATF the opportunity to come out to Mount Carmel and inspect the compound." - David Thibodeaux, one of the survivors

Having obtained the warrants he needed, Aguilera scheduled the raid for February 28, the same day the *Herald Tribune* published the last article in their series, one that included the story of escaped cult member Marc Breault's triumph in getting a 10 year old girl named Kiri Jewell away from Koresh. By this time, the paper had also heard that there was going to be a raid, and thus reporters were there to cover what happened. Lott explained, "One of our reporters had gotten a tip from a confidential informant who told him that they were going to do something, so we made plans to have people out there to cover whatever it was."

The ATF planned to send 75 agents into the compound at once, and it was hoped that they would be able to spread out quickly and take control of the situation. Then they would search the premises and arrest Koresh. Unfortunately, the Branch Davidians were expecting trouble and were ready for the agents. As Aguilera subsequently put it, "I thought the plan had it not been compromised would have worked. ... [When Robert found out he] immediately excused himself, look, I had to leave. David said, no, stay. Robert said, no, I got to go. And as Robert tells me, he walks out the door, and he says, I was just waiting for them to put a bullet in my back. And he said they're looking at us. They know we're coming. You need to call this off. But it was too late, too much had been done and the agents felt that they had no choice but to go forward."

Thus, on Sunday morning, February 28, "Operation Showtime" went into action. 76 ATF agents left the Bellmead Civic Center before the sun came up, headed for Waco in a mile long convoy that featured, among other things, two cattle trailers in which the agents were to hide during the approach to the compound.

They arrived at the compound around 9:45 a.m., and as helicopters buzzed overhead, the agents rushed the building. Aguilera described what happened: "Those that made the initial entry, their concern, where are the children? They had candy bars in their pockets to give out. Chocolate for the kids. Wow. ... A barrage of gunfire just went right through the door. [Agent Roland Ballesteros] died.... How could these guys just start shooting at us?" Clive Doyle, one of the cult members, admitted that some of the Branch Davidians began shooting at the agents: "Suddenly there was some that shot back. We're not denying that. Because they...weren't trusting us and we weren't probably too trusting of them because they were continuing to shoot."

The agents' goal was to capture Koresh, and within the first minute of the assault, three agents made it to his bedroom window before being fired upon. Agent Bill Buford was one of the agents involved that day and later testified, "Initially, prior to exiting the trailer, I heard a tremendous amount of gunfire at the front of the building. It seemed to be all the way across the building, automatic weapons fire, machine gun fire. My team went to the east side of the building, we put our ladders onto the roof. As we were ascending the roof, we received a lot of fire. I could hear the rounds cracking around my head as we went onto the roof. Almost immediately upon getting on the roof, Conway LeBleu, one of my agents, was shot through the head and killed immediately. After he was shot, the Davidians continued to shoot into his body, even though it was obvious he was dead. This happened on several occasions. The window I was going to make entry through, we broke the window out, entered the window and received a withering gunfire on the inside. I encountered one armed individual on the inside. He had backed through a doorway. I went to the doorway and he attempted to enter the room again with an AK-47. I shot and I believe I hit him. He fell. I shot him in the doorway there. Almost immediately. Special Agent Glen Jordan yelled that he had been hit, and I went back to where Glen was. The amount of fire coming into the room was tremendous. I remember thinking I cannot believe I am not getting hit. ... I asked him if he could go, that we needed to get out. About that time, I was shot the first time. A round came through the floor, an M-16 round, I believe. It struck me in the left buttocks and traveled up my thigh and lodged next to my thigh about midway in the thigh."

Obviously, this was not the way warrants were usually served, so most of the agents had never even fired a weapon outside of a shooting range. Now they found themselves in a war zone. Buford continued, "I at that point was knocked back and looked down and observed that this was the arms room as we had thought it was. There were weapons in a gun rack there. There was also a box of hand grenades that I was kneeling beside. And I remember thinking to myself I am glad that those did not go off, because I had to put a distraction device, a flashbang upon going into the room. I again asked Glen if he thought he could go, and the other agent in the room Keith Constantino said he could give us cover. About that time, I was shot twice, once in the hip and once in the upper thigh with an AK-47, I believe. At that point, I realized that I was severely wounded and we needed to get out of the room. I again helped Agent Jordan get to his feet, and Agent Keith Constantino covered for us as we made our way out the window. After I got out onto the roof, I was unable to get to my feet. I rolled off of the roof, fell to the ground and broke several ribs when I hit the ground, and that pain led me to believe that I had been shot again.

However, I had not. Two of our agents dragged me around to the side where they thought I would be out of the line of fire. They…went to get some medical equipment to take care of me. As I laid there, obviously, no threat to anyone, they began to shoot at me again. The rounds were hitting all around my head. I was unable to move because of the wounds I had already received. I was struck in the face at that time with a round, and Special Agent Ken Chism ran over and jumped on top of me and covered me with his body. They then took me around to the side of the building where I remained for the remainder of the firefight, which lasted about 2 1/2 hours."

ATF agent Gerald Petrilli testified about the raid and described his vantage point: "We never made it to the front door of the structure. …the entire front of the compound erupted in gunfire … I heard all the gunfire coming from the compound at us. I saw muzzle flashes. I saw curtains billowing out at the same time I saw muzzle flashes. … There was no way for us to simply get up and walk out without being slaughtered … We were stuck there."

The agents quickly realized that they were in over their heads and withdrew, calling for ambulances and help from the FBI. Byron Sage, one of the Bureau's best crisis negotiators, got there first, a little over an hour after the first shots were fired. He remembered, "The morning of February 28th, 1993, I will never forget. [When] I got there a little after 11:00, [the] gun battle was still raging, which was significant. The average gun battle with law enforcement lasts about two seconds. This was a gun battle that had raged now for well over an hour. … Our top priority right from the start was to get a lid on the violence and then to bring their emotionality down." Bob Ricks, a Special Agent in Charge of the FBI's Oklahoma City Field Office, arrived soon after Sage and agreed, saying, "Bullets were coming out of every window within the compound. [The agents] had the look of defeat, the look of despair, the look of despondency. They had gone through a horrible day and were forcibly required to retreat from that scene."

The task of trying to reason with the Davidians fell to ATF Agent Jim Cavanaugh, who recalled, "We were taking an awful beating. So many men were hurt and wounded and lying down there. When I called the compound, it was Steven Schneider. And he started screaming through the phone that we had no right to be there, to get off the property immediately. I tried to stay calm. I said, Steve, we have to talk. We have to work this out. You and I have to work this out. People are dying. People are hurt. We need to stop the shooting."

Next, Koresh himself got on the phone, leading to the following strange exchange:

> "CAVANAUGH: Everything is OK. Just you and me are talking. And that's the main thing. Because you care for people and then you're sincere and honest.
> KORESH: I care about my father.
> CAVANAUGH: That's right.
> KORESH: My father in heaven."

Cavanaugh later mused, "I had a radio mike in one ear with an agent pleading for his life, and I had this guy on the phone who thought he was God. ... When you drove up, the Davidians opened fire, and I am sickened by any other assertion. We didn't shoot first. We didn't. They shot first. And if I thought that an ATF agent would drive up in front of a structure and shoot, I'd throw my badge in the garbage. It didn't happen."

Cavanaugh and the other negotiators persisted and finally arranged a ceasefire at around 11:30 a.m. By then, four agents were dead and 14 more were injured. A number of cult members were also injured, including Koresh himself, and five were killed, two by their own people.

Both sides later claimed the other fired the first shot. At 4:00 that afternoon, David Koresh released a message to KRLD Radio in which he claimed he and his people were innocent bystanders attacked by the federal government. "They started firing at me and so then what happened was some of the young men started firing on them. They fired on us first."

Less than an hour later, Michael Schroeder, one of the kingpins in the cult's gun business, was shot while returning to the compound.

Around 7:30, Koresh himself did a phone interview with CNN, after which the FBI requested that no more interviews be done because the situation had been classified as a hostage crisis. Nonetheless, KRLD did another on-air interview with Koresh at around 10:00 that evening, during which he devoted his remarks to preaching about his role as a Messiah and claiming that no one else in the compound had been as severely injured as he was:

"REPORTER: Mr. Koresh, how are you doing?

KORESH: (INAUDIBLE)

REPORTER: I understand you've been wounded. Would you describe your position?

KORESH: Weakening.

REPORTER: Are you shot, sir?

KORESH: Yes, I am."

Ultimately, the Department of the Treasury (which the ATF was a part of at the time) concluded in their report on the original raid, "On February 28, 1993, near Waco, Texas, a major law enforcement operation failed. The Bureau of Alcohol, Tobacco and Firearms tried to carry out a flawed raid plan based on one critical element, the element of surprise. Despite knowing in advance that the element of surprise was lost, the raid commanders made the decision to go forward. This decision was brutally exploited by Koresh and his followers. Despite the courageous efforts of ATF agents, four agents were murdered and twenty others were wounded. The vivid and painful conclusion of the operation focused national attention on these events and on ATF. The Review was a response to that public concern."

Chapter 4: Under Siege for 51 Days

"The most disturbing allegation was that we were engaging in child abuse there. The children of Mount Carmel were treasured, and they were a vital part of our small society. Occasionally kids were paddled for misbehaving, but the strict rule was they could never be paddled in anger. The parents did the paddling themselves. Our kids were happy, healthy, and well cared for. The biggest lie, though, is the government's claim that we set the building fire ourselves, to commit suicide. On the April morning when the FBI finally made its move, we had been under siege for 51 days. It was the coldest spring in Texas history that year. The FBI had cut off our power, so we had to heat the building with kerosene lamps. It was kerosene from these lamps and the storage canisters, spilled as a result of collapsing walls and FBI munitions fire, that is cited as evidence that we doused Mount Carmel with an intent of burning it. The 400 rounds of CS gas that the FBI shot into Mount Carmel was mixed with methylene chloride, which is flammable and can explode. The United States and 130 other countries signed the Chemical Weapons Convention banning the use of CS gas in war. Apparently there is no prohibition against its use against American citizens. The amount of gas the FBI shot into Mount Carmel was twice the density considered life threatening to an adult and even more dangerous for little children." - David Thibodeaux, one of the survivors

After the failed raid, a siege around the compound commenced, and the FBI took over in Waco. Jeff Jamar, out of San Antonio, was made the Site Commander, and Richard Rogers, already infamous for his involvement in the Ruby Ridge incident a year earlier, headed the Hostage Rescue Team. Ricks recalled, "Shortly thereafter they were told that we were going to be taking over the handling of the response to the events on that day and that was crushing for them as well." Aguilera explained it from an ATF viewpoint: "At the time, you know, it's personal. You have some animosity. I felt a little, you know, hey, someone is coming in and taking away what I started. But you know, it was for the best because you never know because of what we just went through, what we could have done."

Understandably, the FBI agents who arrived were concerned about what they were getting themselves into. Special Agent Randy Parsons later admitted, "When I first got there, it was a very tense, uncomfortable environment. It was an uncomfortable situation because the Alcohol, Tobacco, and Firearms felt a great sense of loss. It was their own men, their own agents, who were down and were gone." Furthermore, they were dealing with a frustrating character in Koresh. According to Parsons, "Communications opened up pretty quickly. He loved to talk. He loved to hear himself talk. So there was no lack of communication. There was a lack of productive communication." Sage had a similar opinion: "[Koresh] was so calm to a point where we began to immediately start questioning what kind of personality are we dealing with? What we ultimately had come to realize is that we had well over 100 individuals inside of the heavily fortified compound that were there voluntarily because they had backed what they felt was their messiah."

Of course, there were a number of people who were not in the compound voluntarily, and Koresh knew that the FBI's top priority was rescuing the children, so he used that knowledge to his advantage. At one point, he told agents, "There's a lot of children here. I've had a lot of babies these past few years. ... I gave them a message for the radio so that the public can listen to where I'm coming from. And I explained that every time they play it, I would send two of the children out." The FBI allowed the message to be played, after which Koresh did release a number of children and even a few adults.

Once that happened, Koresh told the agents that if they would play one of his sermons on national television, he would come out peacefully: "If they'll show me and show the world what the seven seals are and where they're at in the prophesies, then I will be satisfied and then we'll all come out to you."

For a short time, the agents hoped they had found their answer through this proposal. Sage noted, "That tape was played in the afternoon about 3:00. Went for about an hour and then the clock starts ticking." However, nothing happened until Koresh spoke up and said God had told him to remain inside. Ricks explained, "We're all waiting. We're anticipating. We had buses lined up to receive everybody. ... Now we knew when we had a person who said he was speaking directly to God and God had told him to wait that this was not going to be normal." For his part, Cavanaugh said he believed "that was our last best chance to get him to ever come out. He was fatigued. He was wounded. He was hurt. We had been working on him for three days. But at the very last moment he couldn't do it. He couldn't leave this place where he was God with unlimited sexual favors and walk out to a cold jail cell. He tricked us. He fooled us. He played with us."

The FBI remained focused on rescuing the children, but it became clearer that the Branch Davidians were not going to release them, and Sage described how this colored the agents' attitudes: "That was one of the first and more significant glimpses of the disingenuous nature of how David was dealing with us as far as promises and truthfulness. ... [With one exception] We never got another child out. We've got a total of 21, and I will be eternally grateful for the fact that we were able to accomplish that. ... We continued to press David on that. David finally became very upset with the negotiator, and he stopped and yelled at them. He said, hey, you don't understand. The rest of these children are my children. They're not coming out. The battle of Armageddon was on." The only other child released was a little girl who came out with a note pinned to her jacket saying, "Once the children are out, the adults will die."

The children who had been released, ranging from infants to 12 year olds, told horrific stories of physical and sexual abuse, strengthening the FBI's commitment to arrest Koresh. According to its report to the Attorney General, "On or about March 6, Director Sessions called Gary Coker, Esq., a private practitioner in Waco, to discuss the possibility of Coker acting as a negotiator with Koresh. Sessions explained he decided on his own to contact Coker because, as he said, no one seemed to have the 'key to Koresh.' Sessions said that in his discussions with Coker, Coker said that he had represented Koresh previously (as Vernon Howell), that he was currently representing one of the first women to leave the compound, and that he would walk into the compound to 'pave the way.' Director Sessions recalled that Coker was confident that Koresh was remorseful. Coker told Sessions that Koresh had come from a broken home, and described Koresh as egotistical, messianic, and craving attention. He said that Koresh needed to exert 'strong control,' and that the Branch Davidians did whatever Koresh told them to do. Sessions further recalled Coker saying that Koresh feared going to prison. Sessions noted that Koresh had been acquitted in the earlier shooting case involving George Roden. He and Coker agreed it would be helpful if someone -- perhaps Branch Davidian Wayne Martin, a lawyer -- discussed the fairness issue with Koresh. The conversation ended with Coker offering to speak by telephone with Koresh and to introduce Koresh to the Director. ... On March 12, the first young adults -- Kathy Schroeder and Oliver Gyarfas -- exited the compound. When they called back into the compound, the FBI recorded and later broadcast those conversations over the P.A. system to those inside."

Desperate for more information, the agents hid microphones in cartons of milk they sent in for the children, and they also gave Koresh a video camera so he could record statements made by those in the compound. Naturally, all the video material that came back supported Koresh's claim that everyone was happy to remain with him. Ricks observed, "We really wanted to talk to as many of the children as we could. To see their faces and maybe talk to the mothers if possible, see if they were being held against their will. We were trying to determine what was the nature of the people inside the compound? Were they healthy? Were they suffering? We learned very rapidly that these people came from all walks of life. Some of them very bright people."

Of course, things were even more tense for people in the compound. According to Clive Doyle, who was in the compound throughout the siege, "there was a lot of fear. People were making remarks like, well, if they have got this kind of firepower, if they open up on us, this place is going to look like swiss cheese. People were very concerned that they'd either be shot by the tanks or if the tanks made incursions into the building that we would be crushed by falling timbers and so on."

While the FBI continued to wait and hope for a peaceful resolution, they used various tactics to make things inside the compound as uncomfortable as possible, often playing loud music or shining bright lights in at night. They also cut off both the phones and electricity periodically. Doyle mentioned the effects those tactics had: "And so people like myself who was occupied with various jobs of taking care of garbage, taking care of human waste and so on, throughout the 50 days felt that in all likelihood the women, the children, the elderly would be the first ones out and those of us who were able-bodied and able to take care of necessary chores would probably be the last, but we were sincerely expecting to come out. Everybody I know in there had their bags packed, but as the 50 days wore on, as the tactical team and the tanks began to do things on a more and more — you know, more and more pressure was expended by them, which seemed to work at cross-purposes with what the negotiators were promising and so on, people began to balk. ... We had the electricity turned off, of course, and most of our fresh or frozen foods were destroyed or spoiled. So as I say, we went through varying degrees of hell with noise, music, bright lights. The children were suffering along with the adults. We were without water. Having had our water tanks shot up, we were living on rainwater. Whenever it would rain people would put buckets out the window and collect rainwater. It was rationed. I doubt whether anybody got more than eight ounces a day, if that. I lost 25 pounds by April 19. I know others that lost about the same amount."

Chapter 5: The Tanks Rolled In

"I never heard any discussion of suicide or starting fires. If we wanted to kill ourselves, we would not have waited 51 cold, hungry, scary days to do it. It remains hard for me to clearly remember what happened after the tanks made their move. Walls collapsed, the building shook, gas billowed in and the air was full of terrible sounds: the hiss of gas, the shattering of windows, the bang of exploding rockets, the raw squeal of tank tracks. There were screams of children and the gasps and sobs of those who could not protect themselves from the noxious CS. This continued for hours. Inside, the notion of leaving seemed insane; with tanks smashing through your walls and rockets smashing through the windows, our very human reaction was not to walk out into a hail of death, but to find a safe corner and pray. As the tanks rolled in and began smashing holes in the building and spraying gas into the building, the FBI loudspeakers blared, "This is not an assault! This is not an assault!" It was a very surreal and personal apocalypse." - David Thibodeaux, one of the survivors

Two weeks into the siege, Koresh agreed to send out two of his people to meet with the FBI. Sage explained, "He had selected Steve Schneider, his number one lieutenant, and Wayne Martin, their Harvard-educated attorney, to come out and talk to our representative. The tension was extremely high. You could quite literally feel the crosshairs on him from the Branch Davidian compound, as I'm sure Steve Schneider and Wayne Martin could feel from our tactical teams and had everybody covered."

A few days later, Sage had a very interesting phone conversation with Koresh. "At one point he's talking about my salvation. And I said, David, I am absolutely confident in my salvation as a Christian, and you, partner, are not in a position to judge me. Now that was a very calculated move because stop and think about it. If this individual was delusional and thought that he was Jesus Christ, who is in more of a position to judge me as a Christian than Jesus Christ? But in my mind it had resolved a very critical question, and that is, I did not feel that he was delusional or felt that he was the second coming of Christ. I think that he was a conman and his chosen area of con was religion."

On March 29, Koresh met with Richard DeGuerin, an attorney his mother had hired. According to the FBI's report to the Attorney General, "The following day, DeGuerin again met with Koresh, from approximately 10:00 a.m. until noon, and from 2:00 until 6:00 p.m. Also on March 30, at 3:18 p.m., Steve Schneider spoke with his attorney, Jack Zimmerman, by telephone. DeGuerin returned to the compound on March 31st for approximately five hours. On April 1, both DeGuerin and Zimmerman were inside the compound for eight hours. Three days later, on April 4, they were back in for just over five hours. SAC Jamar said there had been extensive conversations and some disagreement regarding Mr. DeGuerin's access to the compound. Because he thought that any effort to remove the Branch Davidians from the compound peaceably should be attempted, Jamar decided to let him in. Due to the attorney-client privilege, there was no court-authorized Title III monitoring of the conversations that occurred within. DeGuerin did not report anything of value to the FBI after his visits with Koresh and the Davidians. Likewise, Mr. Zimmerman, Schneider's attorney, did not produce any useful information. In SAC Jamar's view, subsequent monitoring of conversations inside the compound revealed that Koresh had used the attorneys to buy time and make it appear that he was interested in resolving the standoff."

By this time, the area around the siege had taken on the look of a circus as all sorts of outsiders began to flood into the area. Branch Davidian supporter David Treibs gave the following account of what happened on April 3, just two weeks before the final assault. "Others were gathering, including men, women, children, and at least 1 baby. Some made their signs. We left around 7:43 am…caravaning to the hill above the roadblock, after picking up Gary Hunt who said he had power of attorney for Koresh. He said this came about because during an interview on the radio which Koresh was apparently listening to, it was asked if K wanted someone come to Mt. C, and if Koresh wanted Mr. Gary Hunt to act as his attorney, or to have power of attorney, and the satellite antenna moved, indicating a positive. … One vendor guy was selling buttons to support the ATF, and was arguing with some in our company that this (Waco) was his area and he supported what ATF was doing and we were wrong. … We met up with folks from Dallas, Austin, and several other places. … It seemed there were more media than us, and more police than us. We had at least 40-50 people, because at least 25 people came from San Antonio. … Some local residents came by just to see what was going on today, to get the latest scoop. Sometime after arrival, some bigmouthed rather obnoxious guy came and started picking arguments with anyone who would argue. John Zimmerman took the bait, and a rather heated, loud discussion ensued. The media quickly flocked around this altercation. People from our side tried to quiet JZ and any others down, saying the dude was an ATF plant trying to make us look like bozos. Someone said the ATF also has sympathizers or plants at press conferences who rescue ATF whenever a good line of questioning was playing out by asking trivial questions." One of the onlookers who came to Waco in March was a young Gulf War veteran named Timothy McVeigh.

Of course, the scene was not a circus but a very dangerous situation seemingly waiting to get out of hand. Treibs remembered, "On arrival at the roadblock we saw brown suited DPS, ATF, Texas Rangers, Waco Police, lined across the road. One ATF guy had an all-black suit and bullet vest. The ATF were in full gear, with bullet vests and either M-16s or AR-15s, MP-5s with both magazines loaded, and shotguns. The ATF each had a sidearm, and most of them had several additional mags for the sidearms. Some of the longarms had mini mag flashlights attached on the business end. ... Some of the ATF were spread out beyond the road, as if to keep us from venturing around the block. They were all holding their rifles, as you would expect in any military operation. ... . Overhead every once in a while a Huey copter with 2 men on each side with their legs dangling off the edge, I could make out 'FBI' on one jacket, each with an M-16/AR-15 or some other rifle watched us. The helicopter landed at one point in the field, and several times flew quite close and slowly around us."

At this point, no one on either side of the argument was accomplishing anything productive. The FBI tried to get things moving by allowing Koresh to speak to his attorney, but this merely proved to be a stalling tactic on the part of the cult leader. Sage explained, "After the attorneys went in, there was -- David said that he was going to write his manuscript of the meanings of the seven seals. ... Finally, on about the 18th of April, the decision was made that we've had enough delays, we've had enough disingenuous lies coming from these individuals. It was time to exercise a tactical resolution."

Indeed, Koresh's estimation on how long the project would take to complete had stretched from two months to a year, and everyone was tired of waiting. Janet Reno, the new Attorney General of the United States, was anxious to be seen as tough and quickly approved the FBI's plan of action. She later said, "I approved the plan and I'm responsible for it. I advised the president, but I did not advise him as to the details." For his part, President Clinton asserted, "Finally, I told her that if she thought it was the right thing to do, she could go ahead."

According to a report subsequently sent to Reno, "The first stage of the operation required two Combat Engineering Vehicles (CEVs) to remove all fortifications, obstacles, and vehicles from the front side of the compound. Double rows of concertina wire were to be placed along the front of the building so that the compound would be completely encircled with wire. On execution of the operation order on April 19, two CEVs were to enter the compound inside the concertina wire prior to sunrise. One CEV would have its boom penetrate the structure on the first floor on one corner and project tear gas.... After delivery, the CEV would withdraw from the structure and stand by. Once the first CEV withdrew, the second CEV would insert additional tear gas into the second floor, on the middle of the right side of the building. The booms were to push aside obstructions and, if necessary, sweep left and right into the windows, making an alternative opening to facilitate the injection of the gas. ... The second stage of the "chemical agent plan" called for the injection of the gas through a corner in the rear of the structure. It was hoped that by introducing gas at opposite ends of the compound, the Branch Davidians would be forced out the front door and surrender. If firing commenced from the compound, the Bradleys [tanks] would be prepared to deliver ferret liquid tear gas rounds into all windows and openings in the compound structure."

One concern constantly on the FBI's mind was that Koresh and his followers would commit suicide, just as the Peoples Temple group had in 1978 under the leadership of Jim Jones. A report to the Attorney General noted, "The input the FBI received regarding the suicidal tendencies of Koresh and his followers was conflicting. …The negotiation team reported its 'growing concern' that, despite his statements to the contrary, Koresh might be planning a mass suicide similar to Jonestown. Nevertheless, the [Behavioral Science Unit] concluded that mass suicide was probably unlikely, because Koresh possessed, among others, the following personality traits: (1) generally acts only in self-interest; (2) statistically shows a low suicide rate; and (3) more likely to arrange a 'suicide by cop' situation than to commit suicide. … The experts who analyzed the letters Koresh sent out between April 9 and April 14 also reached different conclusions regarding the possibility of suicide. Dr. Miron rejected the possibility of suicide…: 'In my judgment, we are facing a determined, hardened adversary who has no intention of delivering himself or his followers into the hands of his adversaries. It is my belief that he is waiting for an assault. . . . Koresh's communication does not resemble the suicidal sermon made by Jim Jones in the last hours of Jonestown. His is not the language of those at Massada or Jonestown. He intends to fight.' However, Krofchek and Van Zandt analyzed the same letter from Koresh and reached a somewhat different conclusion: Koresh was 'willing to kill, to see his followers die, and to die himself [and was] …'fully capable of creating the circumstances to bring this matter to a 'magnificent' end, in his mind, a conclusion that could take the lives of all of his followers and as many of the authorities as possible.'"

Now it simply remained for the FBI to decide when to act. According to Ricks, "We went 27 days with nobody being released. David Koresh became more violent in his rhetoric. He has made such statements as we are ready for war, let's get it on." Thus, on April 19, 1993, the 51st day of the siege, the agents moved in. Sage was given a bullhorn and told to warn the Branch Davidians, telling them, in effect, "David, individuals inside the Branch Davidian compound, we are in the process of placing tear gas into the building. Exit the compound now. Submit to the proper authority, David. You are under arrest. This standoff is over. Believe me, it will not get any better. It will only get worse. David, you have had your 15 minutes of fame. It's time to leave the building."

The final assault began at around 6:00 a.m. that morning, and at first, things went off as planned. The agents were able to breach the compound, allowing them to attempt to flush out the compound's occupants with gas. However, the Davidians managed to resist the tear gas, some by wearing masks and others by hiding in a concrete bunker within the compound.

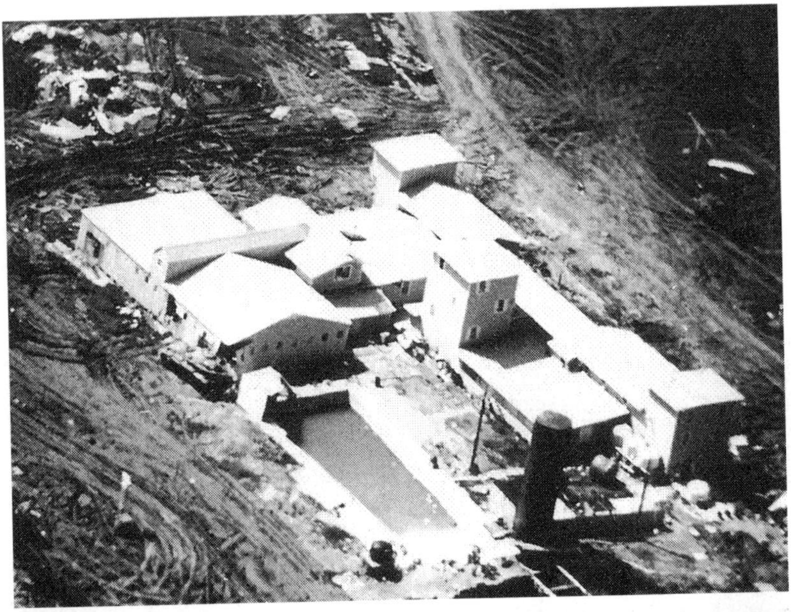

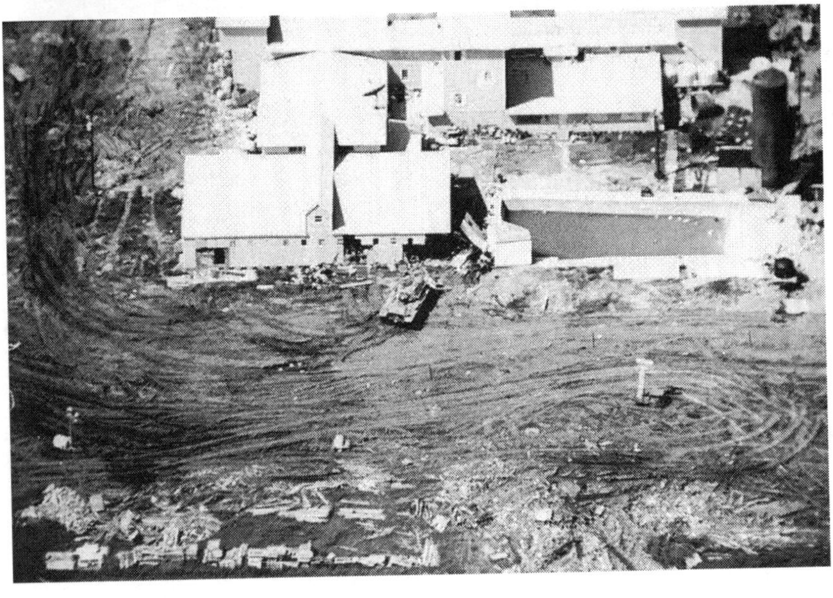

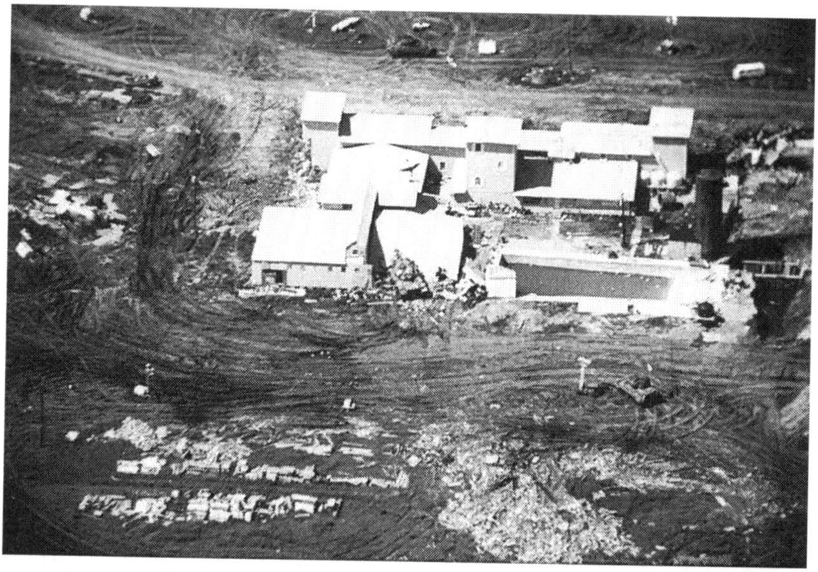

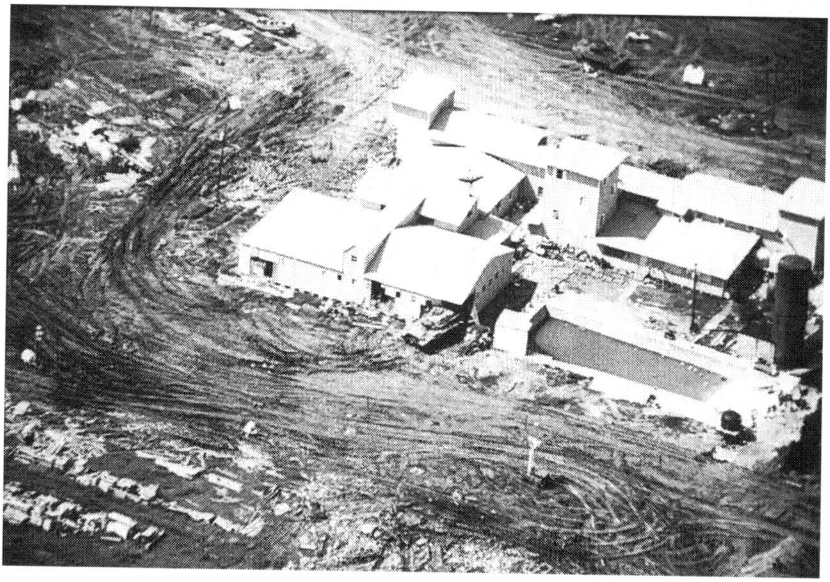

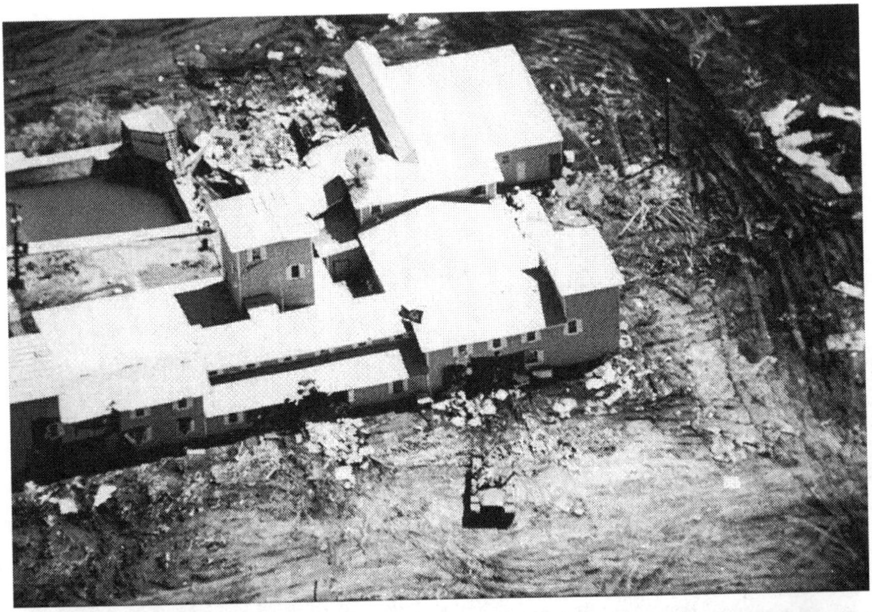

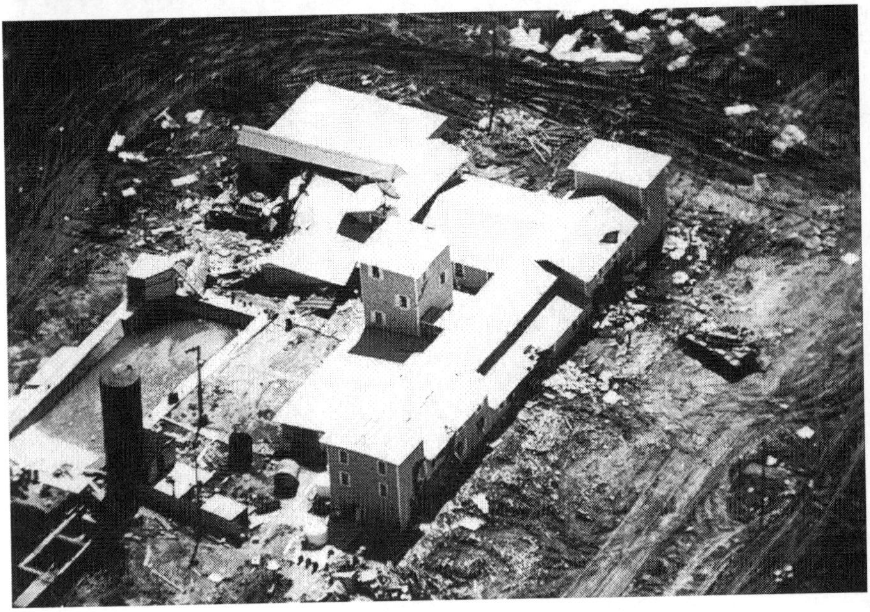

Pictures of a tank breaching various parts of the compound

The Branch Davidians remained in place for nearly six hours, and throughout this time, FBI surveillance devices that recorded comments from within the building indicate that some members were planning to start a fire. Unfortunately, the analysis of the tapes would only come after the confrontation ended because some of the most damning comments couldn't be made out in real time. These included remarks such as "Pablo, have you poured it yet?" "In the hallway" "Things are poured, right?" "Don't pour it all out, we might need some later." "The fuel has to go all around to get started." and "Well, there are two cans here, if that's poured soon." Sometime after 11:30 a.m., other, more obvious comments came through, including "I want a fire." "Keep that fire going." and "Do you think I could light this soon?"

Graeme Craddock, one of the men who escaped the compound, was interviewed by the FBI, and according to the report made to the Attorney General, he told investigators that the Branch Davidians voluntarily started fires: "Craddock advised that when the Bradley came in through the front entrance, they started moving fuel. Craddock believes that the compound had a total of approximately one dozen, one gallon containers of lantern fuel and that they had been located in the lobby area. He said he saw a lot of people grabbing fuel containers and moving them to other areas. Craddock believes that possibly three or four of these containers had been put next to the window that had already been knocked out by the Bradley on the southern side of the chapel area. Craddock said he had heard someone talking about shifting the fuel from the hallway near the chapel to the (northern?) side window of the chapel. . . . He said he had heard someone complain about fuel being spilled inside. ... Craddock indicated that he had heard shouts about starting the fire. ... Craddock said that he did not believe the fire in the chapel was the first fire because before the fire in the chapel had begun, he had seen smoke outside. Craddock also said that he had heard someone say, 'Light the fire,' and that he had also heard someone else say, 'Don't light the fire.'"

Not long after noon, smoke was seen coming from one of the windows in the compound. One Hostage Rescue Team agent told federal investigators afterwards that around 12:10 p.m., "he was able to identify and observe [a] male who was behind a piano inside the front door of the compound. This individual was wearing a dark mask and was carrying a long gun. Seconds after noticing this individual he noticed the man was moving back and forth behind the piano and the individual then assumed a kneeling position. [The HRT agent] noticed the man's hands moving and immediately after that [he] noticed that a fire started in that position. The man immediately departed the area of the piano. At the same time [the HRT agent] noticed a fire start on the red or right side of the building."

Pictures of a fire that started in a second floor bedroom and then spread to a kitchen and dining area

David Thibodeaux, one of the few survivors, recounted the scene inside the compound and blamed the federal agents for the fires: "Around noon I heard someone yell, 'Fire!' I thought first of the women and children, whom I had been separated from. I tried desperately to make my way to them, but it was impossible: rubble blocked off passageways, and the fire was spreading quickly. I dropped to my knees to pray, and the wall next to me erupted in flame. I smelled my singed hair and screamed. Community member Derek Lovelock, who had ended up in the same place as me, ran through a hole in the wall and I followed. Moments later, the building exploded. In the years since the fire, I've tried desperately to find out what really happened. What I've discovered is disturbing. There is convincing evidence that the FBI did more than just create the conditions for a deadly inferno. The disclosures about the use of pyrotechnic weapons and incendiary flares show that they might have actually sparked the blaze. A Defense Department document says that members of a US Army Delta Force unit were present at the siege. The military is barred by law from domestic police work. Infrared images taken from surveillance planes indicate that the FBI was – despite its denials – firing shots into the building and shooting at Branch Davidians who tried to flee. There are photographs that show one of the metal double-doors at the entrance riddled with bullet indentations that could only have come from shooters outside Mount Carmel."

As the fires became visible, Sage began to plead with Koresh: "My instructions over the loudspeakers went from instructions to, please, David, don't do this. David, don't do this to your people. This is not the way to end this. Lead your people out, David. Be a messiah, not a destroyer."

However, it was too late. Once the fires started, the agents acted quickly to try to have them put out, but there was little they could do. According to their report, "Three minutes after the first reports of fire, (12:13 p.m.) the forward command post requested that firefighting assistance be obtained. At 12:15 fire department units were ordered to respond. At 12:34 the fire vehicles arrived and headed straight for the compound. At 12:41 the fire units approached the remains of the building. Although the fire crews did not approach the burning building until 31 minutes after the fire had first been reported, it would not have been safe for them to do so earlier given the reports of gunfire from inside the compound. The FBI has noted that to fight a building fire successfully, firefighters must be able to enter the inside of the building. The FBI has stated that it would have been unacceptably risky for the firefighters to have attempted to approach, much less enter, the burning compound until it was safe to do so. To do otherwise could well have resulted in the deaths of firefighters. Indeed, SAC Jamar stated that even if the firefighters had arrived at the compound earlier he would not have permitted them to enter due to the great risk to their lives. SAC Jamar has also noted that due to the lack of available water in the Mt. Carmel area it would have been extremely difficult for conventional firefighting operations to succeed."

While people continue to debate how the fires started, what is clear is that the fires quickly spread. Aguilera recalled, "Then all of a sudden you see bursts of flames. I'm, like, my god, I hope they allowed the children to leave. ... It was quick. Didn't last very long. The structure of the building was very shadfly made of plywood and it's like a wooden match. ... I did not think that he would fulfill his prophecy. That's what he did. ... I was not just shocked but just horrified. I mean, to think that these children had perished in the fire, and women, and I started asking questions, I'm like, why did this happen? Who started the fire?"

Parsons was also horrified but hopeful that people might still escape: "I will never forget the exact thought that went through my head when I saw the flames. Thank God those mothers will bring their children out now, and we waited and waited and waited, and they didn't bring their children out."

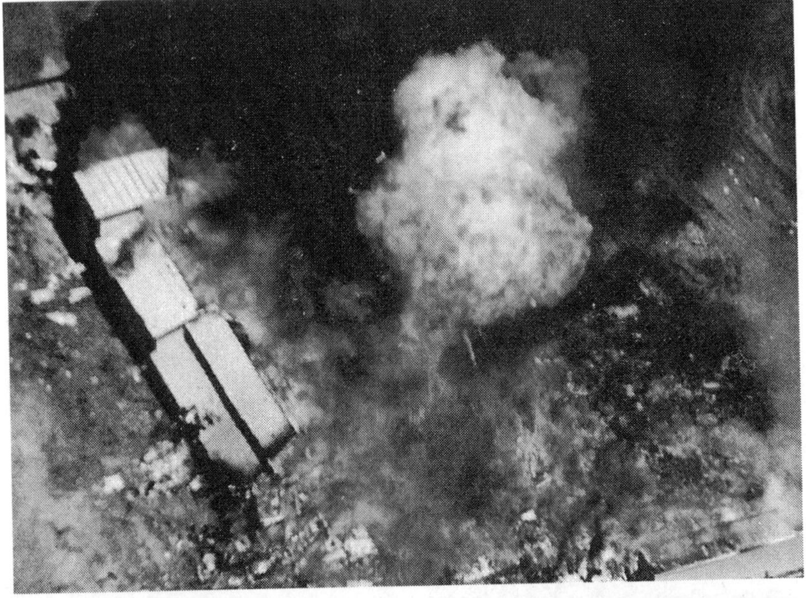

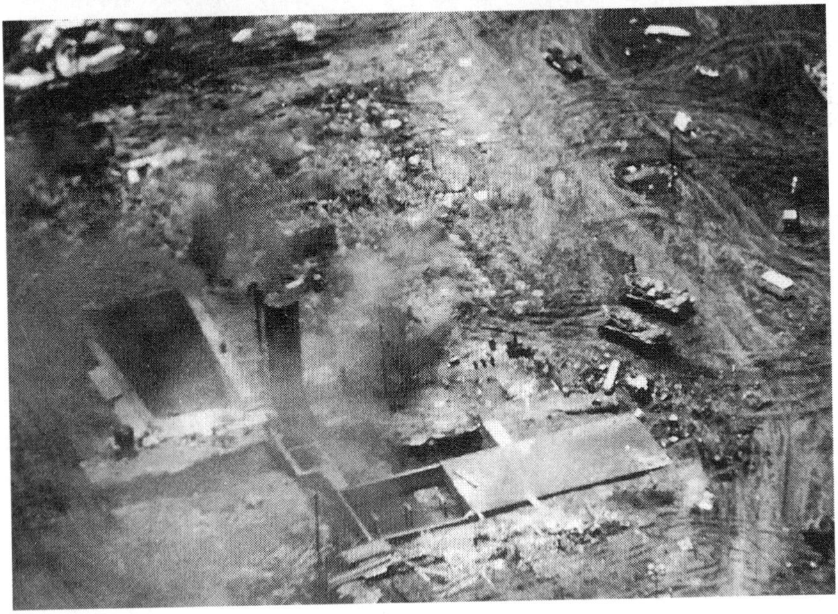

Pictures of the fires engulfing the compound

Sage noted that even as the fires spread, the agents tried to end the standoff: "We never stopped our negotiation efforts. We continued right up until I turned off the speakers on that last day at 12:35 in the afternoon. ... I don't think we, the FBI, ATF, anybody else ever had any control over how this was going end. I think the only control we truly have was when it was going to end. ... We banked on the fact that a parent, if they found their children exposed to that kind of discomfort, would move heaven and earth to get them to a position of safety. And we were wrong. ... But how in the world could they have done that to their kids? Nine people came out, not one of them brought a child."

Clive Doyle was one of the people Sage was talking about; while he escaped, he left behind his teenage daughter, whom he had allowed Koresh to "marry." He later admitted, "You beat yourself up, and why didn't I go looking for one, why didn't I rescue, why didn't I save anybody? I've kicked myself ever since. People do strange things.... Whether anybody actually deliberately lit a fire in there, I don't know. But my question would be, even if they did, whose fault is it? Is it our fault because we were bent on dying or is it FBI's fault for taunting David?"

His remarks were hardly the only accusations subsequently leveled against the FBI and the ATF. Many went so far as to accuse the agents of starting the fire, which infuriated Ricks: "Everyone was in tears. We could all see the faces of the children. We all knew who they were. We had seen them. And that's what we were dedicated to doing, was trying to rescue those kids out of there. And that had all gone up in smoke and we knew that they were all dying and there was nothing that we could do about it. ... It almost became common belief that the FBI had shot the people in there or that the FBI had perhaps started the fire. ... I'm not saying the FBI did everything right or that ATF did everything right. But we did not set the fires, we did not murder anybody."

Despite the anger and conspiracy theories, the evidence was on the government's side. That evidence included infrared images shot by helicopters at the time the fires started. These pictures clearly showed three separate ignition points within the building before any agent ever reached it. Furthermore, as Sage pointed out, "Nine Branch Davidians exited that compound that last day. Seven of the nine had accelerants on their clothing."

Chapter 6: Questions

"Tapes of the negotiations between the FBI and Koresh catch government agents lying about details big and small, as if they wanted the discussions to fail, and wanted only an excuse to attack. There are other questions: Why did the FBI call the local hospital hours before the fire and ask how many beds were available in its burn unit? Why did it not allow firefighters in? What did the FBI negotiator mean when he threateningly said we 'should buy some fire insurance'? Why did the FBI not allow anyone access to the crime scene, despite their promise to the Texas Rangers that they would be allowed to inspect first? Why did they ever raid the compound to begin with, since no charges from the original warrant were ever filed or substantiated? I often wonder why I survived the blaze. Perhaps it was to be some sort of a witness. Federal agents conducted a police raid that wasn't necessary based on charges that would never stand up in any US court. They refused to negotiate in good faith, played horrible sounds of animals being slaughtered for weeks, and finally set our home on fire." - David Thibodeaux, one of the survivors

By 1:00, the fire was out and the compound was gone, as were the lives of 78 men, women and children who had lived there. Ricks claimed, "The children themselves were mostly executed. They were either beat to death, stabbed to death, or shot. ... David Koresh was never going to walk out of that place on our terms. It was doomed from day one that that place, which went by the name of Rancho Apocalypse, was destined to end up in flames." Those who were not shot likely died by their own choice, since there were plenty of routes available for their escape (though a large concrete wall fell on some, killing them or rendering them unable to get out). According to Parsons, Koresh himself was also shot. "It appears as though his second in the command, Steve Schneider, shot David Koresh in the head with a pistol and then Schneider turned the pistol on himself."

The loss of life stirred the American people, and many began to criticize the nascent Clinton administration. Defending her boss, Reno issued an unequivocal statement taking responsibility: "I made the decision. I'm accountable. The buck stops with me and nobody ever accused me of running from a decision that I made based on the best information that I had." For his part, Clinton issued a statement distancing himself from the incident: "I am deeply saddened by the loss of life in Waco today. My thoughts and prayers are with the families of David Koresh's victims. The law enforcement agencies involved in the Waco siege recommended the course of action pursued today. The Attorney General informed me of their analysis and judgment and recommended that we proceed with today's action given the risks of maintaining the previous policy indefinitely. I told the Attorney General to do what she thought was right, and I stand by that decision."

Reno

The controversy around Waco led to a number of civil and criminal trials. 12 of the remaining Branch Davidians were indicted on a variety of charges, including being "part of the conspiracy that Vernon K. Howell, also known as David Koresh, would and did advocate and encourage an armed confrontation, which he described as a 'war,' between his followers and representatives of the United States government. ... David Koresh, originally predicted that this 'war' would occur in the Nation of Israel and later changed the location to Mt. Carmel Compound, near Waco, Texas." The accused were also charged with being "part of the conspiracy that in order to arm his followers for the 'war' with the United States…David Koresh, would and did direct that a business location called 'The Mag Bag' be established near the Mt. Carmel Compound for the purpose, among others, of receiving shipments of paramilitary supplies. The supplies purchased and received at The Mag Bag included: firearms parts (including parts for fully automatic AK-47 and M-16 rifles); thirty (30) round magazines and one hundred (100) round magazines for M-16 and AK-47 rifles; pouches to carry large ammunition magazines; substantial quantities of ammunition of various sizes (including .50 caliber armor piercing ammunition); grenade launcher parts, flare launchers, K-bar fighting knives, night vision equipment, hand grenade hulls, Kevlar helmets, bullet proof vests and other similar equipment."

Finally, there was the matter of the fires. The indictment placed the blame for the fires squarely on the Branch Davidians' shoulders: "It was a part of the conspiracy that on April 18, 1993, Vernon K. Howell, also known as David Koresh, and Steven Schneider would and did finalize a plan to burn the Mt. Carmel Compound in the event an effort was made to finally end the siege by the FBI. This plan was communicated to other residents of the compound. It was part of the conspiracy that on April 19, 1993, the conspirators would and did fire upon tanks and other vehicles manned by FBI agents in an attempt to drive them back from the Mt. Carmel Compound. It was a part of the conspiracy that on April 19, 1993 Vernon K. Howell, also known as David Koresh, would give instructions to spread flammable fuel within the Mt. Carmel Compound upon learning that the FBI was to introduce tear gas into the Compound to end the Siege. It was a part of the conspiracy that a coconspirator would and did give instructions at about noon on April 19, 1993, to start the fires within Mt. Carmel."

Kathryn Schroeder, whose husband Michael had been killed by agents, arranged a plea bargain in return for her testimony. Eight of those tried were convicted and sentenced to prison terms up to 40 years long. Six appealed, and though the court agreed with some of their claims, it did not overturn their convictions. Eventually, the Supreme Court heard the case and cut each sentence by either five or 25 years. By July 2007, every Branch Davidian who was convicted had been released.

On the other hand, those who escaped alive and the families of those who did not filed a number of civil suits against the federal government and a number of other agencies, but their attempts to collect damages did not amount to much.

Faced with no way to correct the past, the government decided to at least learn what it could in order to prevent similar tragedies in the future. The report concluded, "This review of ATF's investigation of Koresh, ATF's attempt to plan and to execute search and arrest warrants at the Compound, and its efforts to 'manage' the aftermath of the raid, provides a rare opportunity to identify what went wrong, to understand the mistakes that were made, and to learn from this experience to make future operations wiser and safer. Although a few in ATF's management saw the Review as an effort to be resisted, the line agents, throughout the process, have been partners with the Review team. They have been cooperative and committed to finding the truth as an essential effort to advancing the professionalism of their agency. In the course of its examination, the Review identified significant failures on the part of a few individuals. But more importantly, it uncovered serious, systemic defects in ATF's ability to plan for and to conduct a large scale, tactical operation in the context of the difficult circumstances confronted near Waco. These shortcomings, however, should not minimize the difficult challenge such a situation presents to all law enforcement...ATF should not be judged by the events of February 28 alone. There is strength, experience and professionalism throughout the agency, and this Review identifies no problems that cannot be corrected. ATF's leadership can take steps to repair the agency's bruised morale and sharpen and refocus its skills on those unique capabilities which have contributed to its pride and its effectiveness in the past. However, to do so the leadership must be committed to positive change and reform. ... ATF's leadership has much to accomplish; they also have much to build upon. Despite the flaws exposed by the events outside Waco, the agency is made up of dedicated, committed and experienced professionals, who have regularly demonstrated sound judgment and remarkable courage in enforcing the law. ATF has a history of success in conducting complex investigations and executing dangerous and challenging law enforcement missions. That fine tradition, together with the line agents' commitment to the truth, and their courage and determination has enabled ATF to provide our country with a safer and more secure nation under law."

Remains of a swimming pool at the compound in 1997

A 1995 picture of the road leading to the compound

A 1997 picture of the entrance to Mount Carmel

A 1997 picture of the remains of a burned bus and bathtub at Mount Carmel

Online Resources

Other 20th century history titles by Charles River Editors

Other titles about Waco on Amazon

Bibliography

Docherty, Jayne Seminare. Learning Lessons From Waco: When the Parties Bring Their Gods to the Negotiation Table (Syracuse, New York: Syracuse University Press, 2001).

Kopel, David B. and Paul H. Blackman. No More Wacos: What's Wrong With Federal Law Enforcement and How to Fix It (Amherst, New York: Prometheus Books, 1997).

Lewis, James R. (ed.). From the Ashes: Making Sense of Waco (Lanham, Maryland: Rowman & Littlefield, 1994).

Linedecker, Clifford L. Massacre at Waco, Texas: The Shocking Story of Cult Leader David

Koresh and the Branch Davidians (New York: St. Martin's Paperbacks, 1993).

Reavis, Dick J. The Ashes of Waco: An Investigation (New York: Simon and Schuster, 1995).

hibodeau, David and Leon Whiteson. A Place Called Waco: A Survivor's Story (New York: Public Affairs, 1999).

Wright, Stuart A. (ed.). Armageddon in Waco: Critical Perspectives on the Branch Davidian Conflict (Chicago: University of Chicago Press, 1995).

Made in the USA
Middletown, DE
11 April 2018